RACE CAR LEGENDS

The Allisons

Mario Andretti

Dale Earnhardt

A. J. Foyt

Richard Petty

The Unsers

CHELSEA HOUSE PUBLISHERS

RACE CAR LEGENDS

MARIO ANDRETTI

G. S. Prentzas

CHELSEA HOUSE PUBLISHERS
New York   Philadelphia

Produced by Daniel Bial and Associates
New York, New York

Picture research by Alan Gottlieb
Cover illustration by Neil Maclachlan

First Printing

1 3 5 7 9 8 6 4 2

Library of Congress Cataloging-in-Publication Data

Prentzas, G. S.
        Mario Andretti / G. S. Prentzas
            p.   cm. — (Race car legends)
        Includes bibliographical references and index.
        Summary   A biography of Mario Andretti, the famous race car driver
    who won the Indy 500 in 1969.
        ISBN 0-7910-3176-4. — ISBN 0-7910-3177-2 (pbk.)
        1. Andretti, Mario. 1940–   —Juvenile literature.   2. Automobile
    racing drivers—United States—Biography—Juvenile literature.
    [1. Andretti, Mario. 1940–   .   2. Automobile racing drivers.]
    I. Title.   II. Series
    GV1032.A5p74   1996
    796.7′2′092—dc20
    [B]   95-8238
                                                                CIP
                                                                 AC

CONTENTS

THE DRIVE TO WIN

What's the most popular spectator sport in the United States? It's not baseball, football, basketball, or even horse racing. America's favorite sport is automobile racing.

To the outsider, it looks simple. You get in your car, keep the accelerator depressed as you hurtle around the track, expect your crew to keep the car in perfect condition, and try not to go deaf as you weave your machine through traffic toward the checkered flag. But in actuality, it's not at all easy. Just as baseball isn't simply a matter of hitting the ball, so racing is full of subtleties.

What does it take to be a world-class race car driver? The more you know about the lives of the greats, the more it becomes clear that each successful driver is an extraordinary athlete gifted with unusual vision, coordination, and the will to win. The concentration necessary to send a car speeding around a track at 200 miles per hour for hour after hour, when a momentary lapse can cause injury or death to him and anyone near the driver who runs is phenomenal. Any driver worth his salt must be strong, self-confident, resilient, and willing to take risks in order to have an opportunity to win.

In addition, racing drivers have to be good mechanics and know how to put together a winning team. They have to find sponsors to put them in competitive cars. The job of a pit crew is to make sure that their car is always in peak performance condition, and all have to be mentally prepared on race day to take into consideration a host of factors such as the other drivers, the condition of the track, and how the car is responding on that day. Without everything right, no driver will stand a chance of winning.

All the drivers in the Race Car Legends series grew up around race cars. The fathers of Richard Petty and Dale Earnhardt were

6

very successful race car drivers themselves. A. J. Foyt's father was a part-time racer and a full-time mechanic; the Allisons and Unsers are an extended family of racers. Only Mario Andretti's father disapproved of his son's racing. Yet Mario and his twin brother Aldo devoted themselves to racing at a young age.

Despite the knowledge and connections a family can provide, few of the legendary racers portrayed in this series met with immediate success. They needed to prove themselves in sprint cars or midget cars before they were allowed to get behind the wheel of a contending stock car or a phenomenally expensive Indy car. They needed to be tested in the tough races on the hardscrabble tracks before they learned enough to handle the race situations at Daytona or the Brickyard. They needed to learn how to get the most out of whatever vehicle they were piloting, including knowing how to fix an engine in the wee hours of the night before a big race.

A driver also has to learn to face adversity, because crashes often take the lives of friends or relatives. Indeed, every driver has been lucky at one point or another to survive a scare or a bad accident. "We've had our tragedies, but what family hasn't?" remarked the mother of Al and Bobby Unser. "I don't blame racing. I love racing as our whole family has."

What each driver has proved is that success in this most grueling sport takes commitment. Walter Payton, the great football running back, and Paul Newman, star of many blockbuster movies, have both taken up racing—and proved they have some talent behind the wheel. Still, it's evident that neither has been able to provide the devotion it takes to be successful at the highest levels.

To be a great driver, racing has to be in your blood.

VICTORY AT THE BRICKYARD

On May 30, 1969, a capacity crowd filled the grandstands and infield at the Indianapolis Motor Speedway to watch the annual running of the greatest spectacle in auto racing—the Indianapolis 500. As a relentless sun beat down on the spectators, local bands played songs that had become a race-day tradition at the Speedway—"Back Home Again in Indiana," "On the Banks of the Wabash,"and "The Star-Spangled Banner." Across the United States nearly one million people jammed into theaters and other venues to watch the closed-circuit television broadcast of the event.

Drivers, crews, and car owners grew restless as the clock slowly ticked toward 11 a.m., the official starting time of the race. At the conclusion of the opening ceremonies, each crew pushed its car onto the track, which is affectionately called "the Brickyard" because it was

At the first turn of the 1969 Indianapolis 500, it's Bobby Unser, Mario Andretti, and A. J. Foyt (left to right) in the lead.

originally paved with bricks. The 33 cars were aligned into 11 rows, three cars to a row. Each driver took a position beside his racing machine.

The three fastest qualifiers—the three drivers who had established the fastest speed during a four-lap qualifying round run earlier in the week—were aligned along the front row. The car of five-time United States Auto Club (USAC) national champion A. J. Foyt sat on the inside of the front row. In his Ford-powered Coyote, Foyt had blistered the track at 170.568 mph to capture the pole position. The intense Texan— having already won the Indy 500 in 1961, 1964, and 1967—was seeking to become the first driver to win the race for the fourth time. Positioned on the outside of the front row was Bobby Unser's car. Unser had won the 1968 Indy 500 and was the defending USAC national champion.

Situated between these two top drivers was Mario Andretti. It was a miracle that the two-time USAC national champion was even competing in this race. During practice sessions earlier in the month, the 29-year-old driver had emerged as the heavy favorite to win the pole position. The Speedway's grandstands and garage areas were abuzz after he turned 171 mph laps in his powerful new four-wheel-drive Lotus. But on race day Andretti was standing beside a two-wheel-drive Hawk, the car that he had driven throughout the 1968 season.

On May 21, the day before qualifying began, Andretti was flying around the track on a practice run. But when he emerged from Turn 4, the rear end of the Lotus collapsed, breaking off the right rear wheel. The car spun one-and-a-half times and skidded 320 feet into the concrete

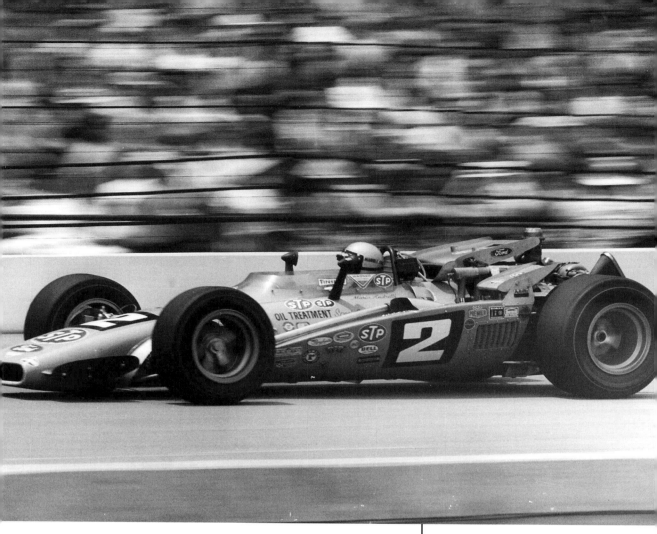

retaining wall. Pieces of the Lotus flew apart in every direction, and the chassis burst into flames. The car ground along the wall for another 60 feet before finally scraping to a halt in the middle of the track. Andretti quickly jumped out of the burning wreckage and was rushed to the racetrack's field hospital. Doctors treated him for second degree burns on his upper lip, nose, and cheeks. Except for the burns, Andretti had escaped from the crash without injury.

Andretti's crew worked feverishly through the night to get his back-up car, the Ford-powered

At one point during the race, Andretti felt a spray of liquid. Thinking the radiator had sprung a leak and his race was over, he started to slow down. Scanning the dashboard, he found the source of the problem: a bottle of Gatorade had tipped over.

Hawk, ready for qualifying. The next day, Mario calmly drove the Hawk through the qualifying run, securing the second spot on the starting grid. As he stood beside his car on race day, the scars from the burns were still visible on his face.

Andretti, Foyt, Unser, and the 30 men lined up behind them had only one goal in mind as they stood beside their cars: winning the Indy 500. The race offered more than double the prize money paid out by any other car race, and the winner could rake in as much as a million dollars from product endorsements and personal appearances. And the winner would emerge as the hero in an epic struggle of man and machine that required more than three demanding hours of driving. The entire drama would be played out in front of thousands of spectators. More people watch the Indy 500 in person than any other single event in the United States—more than the Kentucky Derby, the Super Bowl, or the World Series. Millions of fans flocked to the Speedway during the month of May to watch practices. More than 350,000 spectators jammed into the Speedway on race day. Each driver wanted the fame and glory that belonged to the winner of the Indy 500.

A track official soon gave the signal, and the drivers climbed into their cars. Andretti strapped himself into the seat and covered his blistered face with a bandanna. The temperature was expected to climb up to 85 degrees during the race, which meant that the temperature inside the cockpit would soar to about 125 degrees. The drivers and crews awaited their cue from Tony Hulman, the owner of the Speedway since 1945. Hulman's voice, amplified through loudspeakers, reverberated throughout the Speedway. He carefully intoned the words linked forever with the Indy 500: "Gentlemen, start your engines." The crews helped the drivers fire up their cars and sprinted toward pit row. The howl of the engines was soon matched by the roar of the thrilled fans. The powerful, agile, expensive race cars slowly started moving and quickly settled into position behind the pace car for the warm-up laps.

On the final warm-up lap, the cars glided around the track in perfect formation. As they came out of Turn 4, legendary flagman Pat Vidan waved the green flag, signalling the official start of the race. The cars rocketed down the front stretch and into turn 1. Jamming the accelerator to the floorboard, Andretti nosed his car past Foyt and into the lead. "I just accelerated normally," he later said, "and was surprised no one ran faster."

Although Andretti led the pack, he had little confidence that he would win. In the tune-up runs following qualifying, the car had been overheating. Under track rules, Andretti's crew could not add a second radiator to help cool the engine. Mario decided to run the car all out at the beginning of the race so he could determine how much stress the engine could tolerate. He could then figure out the car's limitations and plan a smart race. "I wanted to see how strong I could run before the thing heated up too much," Andretti later explained. "I felt maybe after twenty, twenty-five laps it would be all over for me."

As expected, after a few laps the dashboard gauges indicated that the engine was overheating. Mario quickly adjusted his speed so the oil pressure and water temperature would drop. On lap 5, Foyt zoomed past him, and soon Roger McCluskey, driving a Foyt-team Coyote, also passed Mario. Andretti took it easy for a while, trying to find the right speed to run. "I found that when the water gauge got to 220 degrees and the oil to 240, it sort of levelled off," he later recounted, "and I could hold it in balance there as long as I didn't run faster, which was around 165, and I just had to hope that was fast enough."

Foyt was out front, flying around the track, and his team-mate, McCluskey, was holding onto second. "It was quite a temptation to race them," Andretti recalled, "but I kept telling myself I didn't dare to." Mario tried to stay close to McCluskey so he could

How grueling is Indy? A month before the 1969 race, Andretti weighed 142 pounds. When he received this congratulatory kiss from Andy Granatelli, he was down to 128 pounds.

draft on the other driver's car and conserve fuel. Meanwhile, the other drivers were trying to catch the leaders. Bobby Unser, who started third, was having handling problems with his four-wheel-drive Lola, but Lloyd Ruby, who had started in 20th place, was charging up through the pack. On the 40th lap, Ruby continued his surge, easily passing Andretti and McCluskey to move into second. Eight laps later, McCluskey coasted into the pits for an unplanned refueling stop, and by the time he got back on the track he was out of contention for the checkered flag.

Andretti made his first pit stop on lap 52. It

lasted an eternity—43 seconds, twice as long as a normal pit stop at Indy. The delay cost him a lot of ground on the track, but it was necessary because the crew had to be sure that he got a full tank every time they refueled the car. By their calculations, the 40 gallons allowed to each driver under race rules would be just enough to finish the race.

When Andretti pulled out of pit row, he was well behind Ruby and much farther behind Foyt. But it was not to be Foyt's day. On the 79th lap, he began having engine problems and pulled into the pits. Foyt's crew worked feverishly to replace the turbocharger. By the time Foyt rejoined the race 24 minutes later, he was too far behind the leaders to win the race.

Andretti streaked into the lead at one point when he passed Ruby, but when Mario made another long refueling stop, 39 seconds this time, he was far behind again. The crucial moment in the race came on the 108th lap, when Ruby went to the pits to refuel. Indy cars are refueled by two hoses that are connected to tanks on each side of the car. The hoses are locked onto the tank to prevent fuel from spilling, which could result in a disastrous fire in the pits. When refueling is complete, the crew disconnects the hoses and the crew chief hits the driver on the helmet or back as a signal to take off.

Ruby's crew chief, however, hit the driver on the helmet before one of the hoses was disconnected. Ruby punched the accelerator, and the car lurched forward. The hose that was still connected to his car ripped out the car's fuel tank. Ruby hit the brakes, but it was too late. The dejected driver got out and walked away, saying to a sportswriter, "I guess it just isn't meant for me to win in this place." Twice before Ruby had been leading the Indy 500 when he was forced out of the race because of mechanical problems.

Suddenly Andretti led the race. The fastest competitors were already out of the race at this point, and the cars closest to Andretti were well back and struggling. But the race was not over by any means. There was still a long way to go— more than 200 miles. If anyone started pressing Mario, he would be forced to increase his speed, which might cause the engine to overheat or the car to run out of fuel.

Andretti was running at a conservative 165 mph, but he was all over the track. His crew flinched every time he drifted too high or too low on the track as he lapped slower cars. On lap 150 as Mario entered turn 3, he got caught in the draft of another car, and the air currents forced the Hawk out of control and pushed it up toward the wall. Fans gasped in unison. "I was sleeping out there, too relaxed." Andretti later admitted. "I didn't expect what happened and it startled me, and the car got out of control and started to slide up into the wall. I was sure I was going to hit the wall, and I just knew that was that and it really shook me, but I steered like crazy and somehow I got it back into control before I hit the wall and straightened out and found my way again and it sort of woke me up."

Mechanic Jim McGee kept flashing a sign with "EZ" written on it as Andretti rolled round and round the oval, and the driver eased off the accelerator. The heat began to get to Mario and the other drivers; the relentless, monotonous circuits around the track began to daze and tire them. Andretti maintained a comfortable lead. The closest competitor, Dan Gurney, was two laps back, Bobby Unser three. All

Andretti had to do was keep going at a reasonable rate, but he was keenly aware of the history of lead cars breaking down at Indy and did not feel secure.

At one point Foyt, who was running several laps behind Andretti, came up behind Andretti, challenging him to race full out. "The temptation was there. It was tough as hell," he later said. But Mario just let Foyt pass; the momentary thrill of competing against Foyt was not worth the risk of making a mistake that could cost him the race. He fought hard to maintain his concentration, focusing on looking for McGee's signals.

Meanwhile, the car's owner, Andy Granatelli, sat in a chair in the front of the pits, waiting. The colorful owner of the STP Corporation had been entering cars at Indy for 22 years but had never won. His cars had been leading the previous two Indy 500s, only to break down in the final laps each time. He was now staring out at the track, counting the last laps.

At last, Andretti saw the white flag, which meant that he was going into his 200th and final lap. The crowd stood and cheered him on. Mario guided the car around the back stretch and through turns 3 and 4, past the wall that he had crashed into only nine days earlier. As he crossed the finish line, Pat Vidan waved the checkered flag with his characteristic flourish. Andretti had completed the 500 miles in 3 hours, 11 minutes, and 41 seconds.

In the pits Andretti's crew was jumping up and down and yelling. Andy Granatelli stood up and bolted toward Victory Lane, where the winning car is parked after the race. The crew followed closely on Granatelli's heels.

When Andretti steered his bright red car into

Victory Lane, Andy was waiting for him. He slapped an STP sticker on the gigantic Borg-Warner Trophy and one on Mario's shoulder. The 300-pound bear of a man wrapped his arms around the diminutive Andretti and kissed him several times on the cheek. The weary driver yelled, "Hey, you're a lousy kisser." Mario's wife, Dee Ann, his parents, and his twin brother, Aldo, joined in the revelry.

Following the celebration in Victory Lane, Andretti met with reporters. When asked about the burns on his face, the weary driver replied, "I guess it hurts, but I was too busy to think about it until now." He discussed the race and how difficult it had been to drive conservatively and how he almost lost it on lap 150. Andretti admitted that he probably would not have won if a fast car had forced him to run the Hawk at higher speeds. He thought that the Lotus might have been the better car but that the Hawk had proven it was good enough. He said that he was now almost glad that the accident had happened, despite the burns. And then a reporter asked the new Indy 500 champion if he might retire. Andretti looked aghast. "No," he retorted. "I'm a race driver, and I'm going to go on driving races."

True to his words, Andretti kept on racing. He never again won an Indy 500 race, but he did come close several times. And during his brilliant career, Mario drove anything on four wheels: midget cars, sprint cars, stock cars, and Formula 1 racers. He matched his skills and nerve with other drivers on dirt tracks, paved tracks, and road courses. No matter what kind of car, what kind of race, what kind of track, Andretti drove to win.

In early 1994, Mario Andretti announced that

Mario Andretti wears the laurels awarded the winner of the Indianapolis 500. Driving a substitute car after a crash that burned him painfully only a week earlier, Andretti averaged 156.867 miles per hour—a new record!

he would retire at the end of the racing season. At each event, racing fans turned out to watch the legendary Andretti maneuver his car around the track. Mario enjoyed his final hurrah, confident that he had always tried his best and proud that his sons, Michael and Jeff, world-class drivers in their own rights, were carrying on the Andretti tradition.

Mario Andretti was born on February 28, 1940, five hours before his twin brother, Aldo. He grew up in Montona, a small Italian town of 3,500 people. Located on the Istrian Peninsula, a thin finger of land in northeastern Italy that points out into the Adriatic Sea, Montona was typical of many small villages in Italy. At that time, donkey carts and horses moved slowly along its cobblestone street, which had virtually no automobile traffic.

The Andretti family was well off by local standards. They owned land, and Mario's father, Alvise Luigi (known to everyone as "Gigi"), was the administrator of seven area farms. Mario's mother, Rina, took care of Mario, Aldo, and their older sister, Anna Maria. Life was simple and fulfilling for the Andrettis until calamity struck.

World War II had broken out in September 1939 when Germany invaded Poland. England

Mario overlooks the Andretti family shortly before they left for the United States.

and France immediately declared war on Germany. Italy entered the war in June 1940 when its Fascist dictator, Benito Mussolini, committed his country's forces to the German side. In 1941, Japan joined Germany, Italy, and the other Axis nations. That same year, the Soviet Union and the United States joined England, France, and the other Allied countries to oppose the Axis powers.

The war tore apart the fabric of life throughout Europe. Although no battles were fought on the Istrian Peninsula, the war devastated Montona. Goods and supplies went to support Italy's war efforts, and shortages became the way of life for all Italians, including the Andrettis.

In 1944, Allied forces overran Italy on their way to Germany. The Allies eventually captured Berlin, and Germany surrendered on May 7, 1945. The war in Europe was finally over. But just when it appeared that the Andretti family could begin to piece their lives back together, the Italian government agreed to turn over the Istrian Peninsula to Yugoslavia, their neighbors to the east, as a condition of surrender. The peninsula had a long history of being a pawn in international politics. Mario's father grew up speaking German because the Istrian Peninsula had been part of Austria-Hungary when he was a child.

Suddenly all of the people living on the peninsula, mostly Italians, were citizens of Yugoslavia. Mario's hometown was no longer Montona, Italy; it was now Motovun, Yugoslavia. To make matters more complicated, Yugoslavia, under the leadership of Tito, had adopted a communist government. Industries were now owned by the government, and farmers had to furnish a large part of their produce to the government. Many Italians, including the Andrettis, were at a loss. They found themselves subject to a foreign government and a political system that they did not like.

In 1948, Tito gave Italians living on the Istrian Peninsula a chance to return to Italy. Concluding that there was no future for their three children in Yugoslavia, Mario's parents decided to leave everything they had and take their family to Italy.

The Andrettis ended up in a refugee camp in Lucca, which is located about 45 miles from Florence. The Andrettis crammed into two small rooms in a building at the refugee camp. To Mario and Aldo, the camp was an adventure. There were many other children to play with, and they soon found a hero—their uncle, Bruno Benvegnu, who also lived in the refugee camp. A veteran of the Italian Air Force, Bruno was handsome and swaggering, and he let Mario and Aldo roar around the refugee camp on his motorcycle. But for the adults life was tough. The best job that Gigi could find was part-time work in a toy factory.

Gigi and Rina were not surprised that their sons loved motorcycles. Mario and Aldo's sister, Anna Maria, later recalled that the twins would pick up plates off their high chairs and pretend that they were steering. A few years later, their great uncle built them a wooden car similar to a soap-box derby racer. Mario and Aldo would tear down the steep hills of Montona in their car, terrorizing neighbors who barely had room to escape on the narrow streets.

In Lucca, it did not take the twins very long before they found a way to be near cars. Mario and Aldo talked the owners of a garage into letting them park cars. The 13-year-olds had never driven a car before and could barely see over the dashboard. "The first time I fired up a car, felt the engine shudder and the wheel come to life in my hands, I was hooked," Mario recalled. "It was a feeling I can't describe. I get it every time I get into a race car." Mario and Aldo zoomed through the streets of Lucca, taking cars from the central plaza to the parking garage.

The twins were soon hooked on motor vehicles. All the boys talked about were cars, motorcycles, and racing. Mario and Aldo soon found a new idol, the legendary Italian racing star Alberto Ascari. In Italy, racing drivers are worshiped by youngsters the same way that baseball, basketball, and football players are worshiped in the United States. But at home the boys had to be circumspect. Their father hated the mention of auto racing, thinking that it was a bunch of foolishness. The boys hid racing magazines under their bed so Gigi would not find them.

Andretti idolized Alberto Ascari (center), shown here after winning the 1953 British Grand Prix.

Good fortune soon shone on the two would-be car racers. A schemer by the name of Count Giovanni Lurani devised a new racing organization that he called Formula Junior. He wanted to give young drivers, ages 14–21, the chance to compete in smaller, less powerful versions of existing Grand Prix cars. The cars would be a little bigger than go-karts. Lurani persuaded the Italian government to finance the operation, arguing that it was the best way to train a new generation of Italian racing champions. "It was a sort of Little League of auto racing, incredibly dangerous," Mario recalled. "Naturally Aldo and I wanted a part of it. They were accepting drivers of fourteen years of age or older. We were thirteen. We lied to get in."

Mario and Aldo were admitted to the program, and only had one more problem—they had no car. But again, good fortune was on their side. The owners of the garage where they worked had bought a Formula Junior car for one of their sons to drive. When the son demonstrated no interest in racing, Mario and Aldo cheerfully volunteered as drivers.

Behind the wheel of the Stanguelini Formula Junior car, powered by an 85-horsepower Fiat Topolino engine, Mario and Aldo began entering and winning Formula Junior races. They traded places driving and had a grand time. They kept their racing a secret from their father, claiming they were going off to Boy Scout camps on weekends when they were actually driving a Formula Junior car that did not have seat belts or a roll bar. When Aldo burned his fingers while playing with the engine, the twins told their parents that a box of matches had exploded in his hands. When Mario broke a kneecap in a crash, he audaciously reported that he had fallen on the church steps.

In 1954, Mario and Aldo went to see the Grand Prix race at Monza, Italy. It proved to be a momentous trip. The Andrettis cheered loudly as their hero Ascari outdueled Argentine driver Juan Manuel Fangio in an electrifying wheel-to-wheel race. "We stood at the end of the straight as it turned into a corner," Mario recalled. "I'd never been able to express it completely, but you can imagine what it meant to me to be that close. Before that time I wanted to be a race driver. After that time, I *had* to be a race driver."

Meanwhile, the Andrettis were living off government welfare payments and what little money Gigi made at odd jobs. Rina's brother, Tony Benvegnu, had been living in the United States since 1909, and, to keep their options open, the Andrettis had applied for an immigration visa. Suddenly, the visa arrived. Mario and Aldo were crushed when they heard that they were moving; they would not be able to pursue their dream of racing glory in the United States. As the family began to pack for their trip, Mario and Aldo made a pact: They would return to Italy when they were old enough and resume their racing careers.

The Italian ocean liner *Conte Biancamano* sailed from Genoa with the Andrettis aboard. On the morning of June 16, 1955, it steamed into New York Harbor and past the Statue of Liberty. After completing immigration procedures, the Andretti family traveled 70 miles to Nazareth, a small town in eastern Pennsylvania. Tony Benvegnu had lived in Nazareth since 1909. The retired coal miner had agreed to sponsor the Andrettis, as then required by U.S. immigration law. The family settled into their new home, and Gigi Andretti quickly found work in a textile mill.

Mario and Aldo were unhappy in their new home. They could speak only a few words of Eng-

Mario Andretti with his brother Aldo (left) at their first race in America.

lish, and their dream of racing heroics seemed an ocean away. The twins moped around for a week until they made an exciting discovery: Nazareth had a racetrack! "That was probably the happiest moment of my life," Mario later remarked. "Instead of looking at racing as something that was way down the road for us, this was something we could begin work on right away."

The Nazareth Speedway was a half-mile dirt oval. It looked nothing like the winding, paved road courses in Europe. And instead of the flashy race cars that the twins were accustomed to seeing in Italy, stock cars—gigantic American passenger cars modified for racing—noisily sped around the Nazareth track. This American style of racing was certainly less glamorous than European Grand Prix racing, but it didn't matter to Mario and Aldo—it was still racing.

Although their racing dreams had been rekindled, Mario and Aldo faced some hard realities in adjusting to life in their new home. The twins were 15 years old, but because of their difficulties with English they were placed in the seventh grade with classmates who were two years younger. The following year, Mario and Aldo were nearly 17 years old and still in junior high.

A teacher recommended that the twins take correspondence courses to earn their high school degree. Mario took the advice and enrolled in a correspondence course. Mario grew close to one of his instructors, Dee Ann Hoch, and they began dating. It took Mario several years to earn his high school diploma. He later commented that he would not recommend correspondence courses to other students. He felt that he missed out on many things by not going to high school.

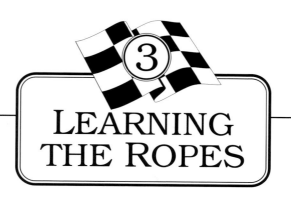

3
LEARNING THE ROPES

Mario and Aldo began to work hard to make their racing dreams come true. Because they could not afford to buy a race car, they decided to build one. It took them three years to learn everything they needed to know about American cars and racing. They hung out at a local garage, went to as many races as they could afford, and peppered anyone who knew anything about race cars with endless questions. They began raising funds to get the car ready. Some of the "investors" in the Andretti race team were friends who chipped in a whopping $5 apiece. A $350 loan from a local bank also helped. All along the Andretti boys tried to make sure that their father did not hear about what they were up to.

The first race car that the Andrettis built was a 1948 Hudson Hornet. When the 1959 season at Nazareth Speedway opened on April 25, the

Andretti at Nazareth Speedway in 1959 with the third car he ever raced: a modified 1937 Hudson.

twins realized that they still had a problem. "One car, two of us," recalled Aldo. "We decided to flip a coin for who would take the first race, and we would take turns after that." Aldo won the coin toss and jumped behind the wheel. Starting in the back of the grid, Aldo blistered past the field to win the race. The Andrettis gleefully ran to the pay window to receive their winnings—$90. The next week, Mario stood on the accelerator and guided the Hornet through the field to win the race. The twins rang up another $90.

The Andretti boys kept winning races, but track officials soon decided to move them from the sportsman class races to the more competitive modified class races. They ran well but did not win any races in the higher class. "There is no doubt that we were going too fast too soon," Mario later observed. "We had no idea how to drive—how to pace a race. We just revved it up and stood on it—and who cares about anybody or anything that got in our way."

The final race of the 1959 season at Hatfield, Pennsylvania, was a 50-miler for modifieds. In the first heat, Mario qualified for the feature race in a 1933 Ford. In the second heat, Aldo was at the wheel of the Hudson. He was running in third place, good enough to qualify for the feature, when disaster struck. Going all out trying to catch the leaders, Aldo hooked a guard rail, and the Hudson tumbled end over end down the track. When Mario reached the car, Aldo was unconscious.

An ambulance raced Aldo to a local hospital. Mario was terrified. He was not sure whether Aldo would live, and he knew that he would have to tell his parents about the accident. When Gigi heard the news he was livid, saying that he knew all along that this racing business would be trouble and that Mario and Aldo had disgraced the family. Returning to the hospital the next day, Mario learned that his brother's condition had worsened. X-rays revealed that Aldo had a skull fracture, and he had slipped into a coma.

Mario maintained a constant vigil at Aldo's bedside. After two weeks Aldo's eyelash started moving, and he soon opened his eyes. His first word were: "I'm sure glad you were the one who had to go home and face the old man." After another month, Aldo was well enough to return home. But he was still in bad shape. Aldo left the hospital weighing only 90 pounds, 70 less than he had weighed six weeks earlier, and he had to relearn how to walk and write.

In the meantime, Mario had salvaged some of the parts from the crunched-up Hudson, including the engine, and installed them on a 1937 Hudson chassis. Gigi saw the boys hanging out with their new race car at a local garage. When they returned home that day, he laid down the law, "You can live here. But there will be no words spoken among us." For six months, Gigi refused to talk to his sons.

The tension at home upset Mario, but not enough to keep him from racing. At the beginning of the 1960 season, he had four straight wins. Then Aldo announced that he was ready to race again. Mario felt that his brother had not fully recovered and tried to talk him out of returning so soon. But Aldo was adamant, and he entered a race.

Once the race began, Mario immediately saw that Aldo was having trouble controlling the car and was running too close to the fences. In what seemed like a recurring nightmare, Mario watched helplessly as Aldo hooked a guard rail. When the car went airborne and tumbled end over end, Mario felt sure that his brother had killed himself. Aldo emerged from the wreckage with only a bloody finger, but he decided that he should take it easy for a while.

While Aldo continued his recovery, Mario's racing career began to advance. Like major league baseball, auto racing has its minor leagues. Drivers usually start racing motorcycles or sports cars and slowly work their way up to more competitive forms of racing. Mario started working his way up on small tracks throughout the Northeast and the Midwest.

In 1960, Mario began driving a stock car sponsored by a construction company. He also got involved in sprint car racing, which was a big step up. His first sprint car ride was in a racer from the late 1940s that had a Cadillac engine and virtually no brakes. He competed in his first sprint race in West Lebanon, New York, finishing in eighth place.

During 1960 and 1961, Andretti entered 46 stock car races and won 21—a strong performance. But on the more difficult United Racing Club (URC) sprint car circuit, Mario managed to finish only about half of the 20 races that he entered. And his eighth-place finish at West Lebanon was his best finish of the year. Although he wasn't winning any races, Andretti was gaining an abundance of experience.

Andretti wanted to drive bigger and better cars, but no one would give him a chance. He soon figured out the problem: Car owners thought that he was too small. Many racing people believed that drivers had to be big, strong men to handle powerful racers. Mario constantly got

inferior cars because owners did not trust the scrawny 21-year-old with their best cars. (In a few years, Andretti's size—5'5", 135 pounds—would became an advantage when rear-engine cars, which have very small cockpits, began to dominate races.)

Meanwhile, the relationship between Mario and Dee Ann Hoch blossomed, and the couple married on November 25, 1961. With financial help from his father-in-law, Andretti bought a three-quarter midget racer and began racing in the indoor winter circuit.

Midget car racing is frenzied. Many cars compete in each heat, and the congested track inevitably becomes a havoc of spins and crashes as the cars dash toward the finish line. Andretti did not do very well on the midget circuit until he won his first race on March 3, 1962. The victory in the 35-lap feature at Teaneck, New Jersey, boosted his confidence, and he won three

The start of a famous rivalry: Mario Andretti (left), in his first USAC race, faces off against A. J. Foyt. The brakes on Andretti's car failed, and he was not able complete this 1963 sprint-car race.

more races before the end of the season. Mario competed in 33 midget races that season, winning four and finishing in the top ten 24 times. The young driver from Nazareth did not make much money, but he was beginning to build a reputation for himself.

Andretti's performance on the midget circuit attracted the notice of Bill and Eddie Makata, who owned a racing team based in Maplewood, New Jersey. The Makata brothers asked Mario to drive their Offenhauser midget for the 1962 summer season. Andretti accepted the offer and won his first outdoor midget race in Hatfield, Pennsylvania. Andretti and the Makata brothers worked well together, and Mario drove about 80 midget races for them in 1963. But Andretti was not satisfied. He was still in the minor leagues, and when a better opportunity came along, he left the Makata team.

On September 21, 1963, Andretti drove in his first USAC race, a sprint car race at Allentown, Pennsylvania. Sprint car racing is perhaps the most dangerous form of racing in the United States. The small cars have powerful engines and are highly maneuverable. The races are usually run on dirt tracks, which get bumpy after the racers have completed a few laps. The lightweight cars easily go airborne when they hit a rut, and many drivers have been killed in sprint car races.

Entering his first sprint car event, Andretti was one step closer to the big leagues, competing against A. J. Foyt and other top drivers. Mario was the fourth fastest driver in the qualifying round, but soon after the flag dropped for the 30-lap feature, the brakes on his car went out. Andretti had to withdraw from the race, but

Mario is about to crash in this 1965 sprint car race, at Terre Haute, Indiana. He would be fine, but the car was totally destroyed.

he was awarded 14th place. In a race two weeks later, Andretti finished in 13th place. He was not thrilled with the poor finishes. Mario comforted himself, however, with the knowledge that he had gotten the most out of the car, and he savored the first taste of competition against the big boys of USAC.

During this time, Andretti was only a part-time race car driver. He also held down a day job, working as a foreman at Motorvator, a company in Nazareth that made golf carts. Motorvator's owner was a friend of Mario's, and he gave the young driver as much time off as he needed to pursue his dream.

In April 1964, Andretti got an offer to drive in the Trenton 100. It would be his first USAC championship race—the major leagues of auto

After watching Andretti race, legendary crew chief Clint Brawner (left) told his wife he was "tired of going with these old guys that have been around a long time and [would] try another new kid and spend about a year with him."

racing in the United States. The Trenton oval was paved, a real treat for the young driver. On race day, however, an on-and-off drizzle made conditions on the smooth asphalt extremely treacherous, especially for Mario, who was behind the wheel of a car with poor brakes. Andretti labored home in 11th place.

Andretti anxiously awaited a call to drive in the 1964 Indianapolis 500, but his telephone did not ring. It was beginning to look as if he would have to return to the minor leagues when respected car owner Rufus Gray called to ask Mario if he would be interested in driving one of Gray's sprint cars. Andretti knew that this opportunity could be a turning point in his career: If things worked out, he could become a full-time driver. But joining Gray's racing team meant that he would have to give up the security of his job at Motorvator. Mario talked over the situation with his wife. "This is what you want," Dee Ann told him. "If you believe it is the opportunity you've been waiting for, you should take it." That was exactly what Andretti wanted to hear, and he immediately called Gray to accept his offer.

Andretti's first sprint car race with Gray was to be a big event on the dirt track at Salem, Indiana. Because practices for the nearby Indy 500 had already started, many big name drivers were slated to compete in the race. The race was scheduled for May 3rd, but heavy rain forced its cancellation. Mario returned to Indiana at the end of the month to attend the 1964 Indy 500 as a spectator. He realized that he was not ready to compete at the Brickyard yet, but he wanted to look, listen, and learn.

The rescheduled Salem race was finally run, and Andretti finished in fourth place—an impressive feat for a young driver. In a stroke of good fortune, Mario was in the right place at the right time when legendary crew chief Clint Brawner was looking for a driver for his championship car. His driver, Chuck Hulse, had been injured in a sprint race and was out for the season. Brawner went to watch the young kid from Nazareth whom he had heard so much about compete in a sprint car race in Terre Haute, Indiana. Brawner and the rest of the paying customers got their money's worth watching Andretti duel A. J. Foyt. The older driver won the race, but Andretti was impressive.

Brawner told Andretti that he had potential and would like him on the Dean Van Lines team. He wanted Mario to take it easy at first—to learn the ropes. The experienced crew chief told Andretti that they were going to skip the next championship race, which was to be held at Langhorne, California. At the time, the D-shaped dirt track was considered by everyone to be the most dangerous course on the championship circuit. Brawner did not want his inexperienced young driver to mess up the car—or himself—at Langhorne.

Andretti, however, wanted to prove that he could handle the track and found another owner who needed a driver for the race. Mario's bravado turned to terror soon after the green flag dropped. The young driver was scared stiff as he maneuvered the car around the hazardous track. He was happy to finish in ninth place; he was overjoyed to still be alive.

The next race, the Trenton 150, was Andretti's first race with the Dean Van Lines team. Brawner had the car purring, and Mario was running in sixth place when he hit an oil slick on lap 78. The car spun all over back stretch, but Andretti avoided hitting anything. He got the car started again and finished in 11th place. At the next circuit stop, the Milwaukee 200, Mario finished third in his front-engined Offenhauser. This race marked a significant turning point in racing history. The new rear-engine Fords made their debut that day, and they stole the show by placing nine cars in the top ten finishers. It signalled the beginning of the end of the front-engined Offenhausers, which had been the dominant race car for years.

Between stops on the championship circuit, Andretti continued driving in the USAC National Sprint Car division. He had been finishing near the front in the Rufus Gray car all season but had not captured a single checkered flag. Then on October 4, Mario won his first sprint car race—a 50-miler at Salem, Indiana. He and the crew celebrated his first USAC victory.

By the end of the 1964 season, Andretti had finished in the top ten in five races and had picked up enough points to finish 11th in the USAC championship point race. It was a remarkable feat because he had not raced for the entire season. To top off his impressive rookie year, Mario finished third in the USAC sprint car standings.

Going into the 1965 season, Andretti worried that he would lose his job. He had joined Brawner's operation as a substitute driver, but because of his success, he felt that he should be Dean Van Lines's full-time driver. Mario presented his demands to Brawner, who agreed to keep Andretti as his sole driver. The young driver would receive $5,000 a year and earn 40 percent of the winnings.

In the first race of the season, the Phoenix 150, Andretti led the race for 63 laps—the first time he had ever been in front in a USAC championship race. On the 110th lap, however, while trying to avoid Johnny Rutherford's spinning car he lost the lead to Don Branson and ended up finishing in sixth place. At the next race, the Trenton 100, Mario finished second behind Jim McElreath.

The next big race on the USAC calendar was the big daddy of them all—the Indianapolis 500.

Dee Ann Andretti smiles at Mario after his victory at the 1967 Hoosier 100.

The month-long preparation for the race always drains drivers and their crews. Tension mounts with each passing day, especially for rookie drivers. Andretti was not the only rookie driver who showed up at the Brickyard in 1965. Gordon Johncock, Al Unser, and Mickey Rupp were among the young hot shots who also arrived for their first try at Indy.

Rookie drivers must pass the rookie test before they are even allowed to run in the qualifying rounds. Andretti had no trouble with the test, passing it with flying colors. But next came the really hard part—qualifying for the race. Only 33 cars can run in the Indy 500, though easily twice that number may compete during the four days of qualifying. This puts tremendous pressure on experienced drivers as well as rookies. The car with the fastest four-lap time trial on the first day of qualifying captures the pole position.

Andretti, the 11th driver to take the track, quickly made a name for himself by posting a 158.849 mph time, breaking the track record. But three other drivers—A. J. Foyt, Jim Clark, and Dan Gurney—later posted better times. Still, Andretti was overjoyed with his effort. Not only had he qualified for the race, but he would be starting in the second row.

From his fourth-place start, Andretti quickly fell back to fifth place. He soon realized that he could not keep pace with the top four cars but felt that he could outrun the cars behind him. After about 20 laps, he had settled into a rhythm. Jim Clark, the British driver in the lead car, ran away from the field. Foyt and Gurney dropped out with mechanical problems, which left Mario in third place behind Clark and Parnelli Jones.

Andretti and crew worked late into the night rebuilding and checking his car before his first Indianapolis 500 in 1965.

Andretti tried to catch up with Jones but came across the finish line six seconds behind the veteran driver. The heat in the cockpit had blistered Andretti fingers, and he was so exhausted after the race that he had to be pulled from the cockpit. But Mario's third-place finish, along with his fourth-place qualifying run, easily won him the Indy Rookie of the Year award. He also shared the $42,551 third-place prize money and racked up 700 points in the race for the USAC season championship.

Mario's strong finish at Indy was just the beginning of a phenomenal season for the young driver. He won only one race, a 150-mile road

At the 1966 Phoenix 200, Bobby Unser has a minute lead over Mario Andretti—but Andretti would come back to win the race.

race at Indianapolis Raceway Park, but he finished strongly in many races, including seconds at the Langhorne 100, the Atlanta 200, the Milwaukee 150, and the Phoenix 200. Andretti had one of his worst days at the Trenton 200 in September. He finished in 13th place, but with only two races remaining in season no one could catch his point total for season. He became the first rookie to win the USAC national championship since 1949, when Johnnie Parson accomplished the same feat.

Hot off of his championship season, Andretti started the 1966 season with high hopes. But in the first race of the season, Mario and A. J. Foyt were battling it out for the lead when they crashed into each other while trying to pass slower traffic. Bad luck continued to haunt Andretti. At the Indy 500, he qualified for the pole position at 165.899 mph but had to drop out of the race in the 17th lap when a twisted rod trashed the engine.

The tide soon turned. Andretti led the next three races—the Milwaukee 100, Atlanta 300, and Langhorne 100—wire to wire. For an amazing 500 consecutive miles, he made all of the other USAC championship drivers eat his dust. Mario then won a road race at the Indianapolis Raceway Park for his fourth victory in a row. Later in the season he won the Milwaukee 200 and the Trenton 200. He clinched his second national title by finishing 11th in a 100-mile dirt race at Sacramento. To top off the season, Andretti won his final race of the year, the Phoenix 200.

After two straight national championships, Andretti felt like the king of the racing world. He won the 1967 Daytona 500, the biggest race of the NASCAR circuit. Behind the wheel of a Ford Fairlane, Mario grabbed the lead for good at the 200-mile mark and pushed the stock car around the 2½ mile oval to take the checkered flag. He followed up that impressive victory by jumping behind the wheel of a sports car at the 12-hour endurance race at Sebring, Florida. In a Ford Mark IV, Andretti and co-driver Bruce McLaren covered 2,376 miles in 12 hours, breaking the old speed record en route to the victory.

The 1967 Indy 500 witnessed the debut of Andy Granatelli's new turbine engine, which set the racing world abuzz. Andretti ignored all the talk about the powerful new car and captured the pole position with a record speed of 167.942 mph. But on race day, Mario lost a wheel on the 58th lap and ended up in 30th place. Meanwhile, Parnelli Jones was running away from the field in the Granatelli car. But four laps from the finish, a $6 ball bearing in the gear box froze and took the $250,000 car out of the race. A. J. Foyt cruised to his third Indy win.

Following his disappointment at Indy, Andretti drove in the legendary 24-hour endurance race in LeMans, France. An error by the pit crew caused his car's brakes to lock up, and in the resulting crash Mario broke his ribs. Three days later, Andretti was back behind the wheel at a race at Mosport, Canada. He hit an oil slick, spun out of control, and rammed into a bridge abutment. He broke the same ribs. Despite the pain, Andretti raced in a 100-mile race at Langhorne the following day. Amazingly, he finished third.

Andretti then reeled off six victories, winning the 150-mile road race at Indianapolis Raceway Park for the third year in a row, a 150-miler at Langhorne, and 200-milers at Milwaukee, Phoenix, and St. Jovite, Canada. Entering the last race of the season, a 300-miler at Riverside, Mario was within reach of a third national championship. He stood in second place behind A. J. Foyt. Andretti finished the race in third place, but Foyt finished fifth and won the USAC championship.

Before the 1968 season began, Al Dean, owner of the Dean Van Lines racing team, died, and Andretti bought the assets of the team. Although his car had a new turbocharged Ford engine, Mario had a string of poor finishes. The new engine provided a lot of horsepower, but it bogged down coming out of corners and had carburetion and overheating problems. Andretti dropped an older Ford engine into his car while the Ford engineers worked to improve the new engine before the Indy 500. With the old engine, he finished second at the Trenton 150 in April.

At the 1968 Indy 500, the rules battle over the new generation of turbine engines overshadowed the race. Many owners wanted the

Andretti (#11) goes to the outside in order to pass at the 1967 Daytona 500.

engines banned, but the USAC rules committee, seeking a compromise, placed a size limitation on the turbines that lowered their performance. Andretti qualified in fourth place but burned out a piston in the first lap of the race. He jumped into the team's second car, driven by Larry Dickson, but after 28 laps, the engine in that car conked out also. Bobby Unser coasted to victory when Granatelli's turbine car, driven by Joe Leonard, dropped out with a broken fuel pump shaft on the 191st lap.

Andretti finished second in six of the next nine races and won the Trenton 200. Andretti had steadily racked up points in the national championship race. Going into the final race of the season at Riverside, Mario had the most points, followed by the Unser brothers—Bobby and Al.

Andretti's car developed engine troubles, and he finished way back in the pack. Bobby Unser finished second and won the national championship by 11 points over Andretti.

Before the 1969 season began, Andy Granatelli offered to buy Andretti's team. Tired of all the headaches involved with being the team's owner, Mario gladly accepted. The new team planned to race a Ford-powered Lotus, but the car would not be ready for the start of the season. So Andretti drove his old car, a Hawk that was powered by a turbo-Ford engine. At the Phoenix 150, the first race of the 1969 season, Andretti had logged only 29 laps when he had to withdraw from the race with a burned-out clutch. He bounced back by winning the next race, a 200-miler at Hanford. It marked the first championship victory for Andy Granatelli in his 23 years of racing.

The new Lotus arrived in time for the month-long preparation for the Indy 500. The crew had the car running smoothly, and many track insiders thought that Andretti was a lock to win the race. On the final day of practice, however, a rear wheel flew off the car, and Mario crashed into the wall. Although he suffered burns on his face, the determined driver returned to the track the next day to qualify for the second starting position in the Hawk. Although the car had some cooling problems, Andretti won the race easily after other top contenders dropped out or fell behind early.

With the Indy victory under his belt, Andretti began the quest to win his third USAC national championship. On June 29, Mario competed in the unusual 12½-mile Pike's Peak hill climb—a wild and woolly race up a treacherous, windy mountain road to the top of Colorado's most famous mountain. Although the race had been dominated by the Unser family for 40 years, Andretti once again showed his versatility. Behind the wheel of a Chevy, Andretti streaked up the mountainside and won the race.

Andretti then returned to Nazareth for Mario Andretti Day. The town threw a rollicking two-hour parade to pay honor to its favorite son. Later, at a party at his house, Mario jokingly commented, "Many people here in town thought I'd never amount to anything. Maybe they were right. Here I am at twenty-nine and I don't have a steady job."

At the Trenton 300, Andretti edged out Bobby Unser to win his 26th championship race. The victory assured him of his third USAC championship, but he still had something to prove. The final race of the season was the Rex Mays 300 at Riverside, California. Mario had never won on that track, and with the national championship already in his back pocket Andretti was determined to win the race. He staged a thrilling come-from-behind sprint and pulled away at the end to win by thirty-seven seconds. The victory capped Andretti's finest year. He won the national championship by largest point margin ever, racking up 5,025 points. Al Unser, the second place finisher, had only 2630.

THE MAN WHO COULD WIN ANY KIND OF RACE

F or Mario Andretti, the highlight of the 1970 season was the grueling noon-to-midnight race at Sebring, the oldest endurance race in the United States. He had won the race in 1967, but this year was special because the Italian-born Andretti was driving for Team Ferrari. Andretti put the Italian sports car on the pole position with a record qualifying speed of 121.954 mph. Alternating with Italian driver Arturo Merzario, he led for 500 miles and had a 50-mile lead when the car broke down. He jumped behind the wheel of the other Ferrari team car and sped onto the course in fourth place, with only 45 minutes left in the race.

Driving like crazy, Andretti quickly passed the third- and second-place cars and zoomed past the lead car with 19 minutes to go. Running low

Mario Andretti and his Lotus (rear) came on to win the 1976 Japan Grand Prix. Alan Jones's Surtees took fourth place.

Andretti takes the checkered flag at the 1977 Formula 1 race at Monza, Italy.

on fuel, he made a quick pit stop. Burning rubber as he left the pits, Andretti managed to get the Ferrari back on the course just ahead of a Porsche driven by Peter Revson. Mario held off Revson for the final laps to take the checkered flag in the closest race in Sebring history.

The following year, Andretti began to pursue his lifelong dream, racing on the international Grand Prix circuit, also known as Formula 1 racing. The Grand Prix circuit consists of 16 races held over 10 months on four continents. It provides the ultimate test of a driver's skill and courage. Mario had previously raced in two Formula 1 races but had not finished strongly. He decided to devote more of his time to the Grand Prix circuit.

Andretti's concentrated effort paid off. He won two Formula 1 races in 1971: the South African Grand Prix at Kyalami and a Grand Prix race at Ontario, California. The South African race victory was particularly sweet because he won at the wheel of a Ferrari, the same make that his childhood idol, Alberto Ascari, had driven.

That same year Andretti parted company with Andy Granatelli and joined a new USAC racing team put together by former driver Parnelli Jones. The two other drivers on the team were Al Unser and Joe Leonard. Racing writers dubbed it "the dream team," but everyone's high expectation never materialized. The cars did not run very well, and Andretti, Unser, and Leonard never found their way to Victory Lane.

Andretti left Jones's team in 1976 to join the Grand Prix circuit full time, although he occasionally drove in USAC races for the Roger Penske team. Mario signed with Colin Chapman, whose Lotus team was building a new Formula 1 car—the Lotus 79. Andretti had driven for Lotus in his first Grand Prix race in 1968, and he had great respect for Chapman's abilities as a car builder and team manager. He believed that the Lotus 79 would be a superb race car.

The Lotus 79 was not close to being ready for the 1976 season, so Andretti climbed into the cockpit of the existing Lotus model. Even though he was driving an older car, Mario finished in sixth place in the 1976 Grand Prix points standings and won one event, the Japanese Grand Prix. In 1977, Andretti continued driving the older Lotus while testing the Lotus 79 to get it ready for the 1978 season. He won four Grand Prix races in 1977—in Spain, France, Italy, and

Long Beach, California—and finished third in the year's point championship.

The 1978 Grand Prix season proved not only Andretti's greatest year, but one of the greatest years any racer has ever put together. He won the first race of the season in Argentina and then swept through the European events in Belgium, Spain, France, and Germany. He also placed second at Long Beach and fourth in Brazil. Despite this impressive achievement, he did not have the season championship sewn up. Mario had earned 54 points (first place earns 9 points; second place, 6, third place, 4) going into the Holland Grand Prix. Several top drivers— France's Patrick Depailler (32 points), Argentina's Carlos Reutemann (31), and defending champion Niki Lauda of Austria (31)—were still in contention.

Andretti's closest competitor, however, was his teammate, the Swedish driver Ronnie Peterson. All year, Peterson had been the ultimate team player, pacing Mario and running interference for him whenever the older driver was in the lead. Although Peterson was given the green light to win only when Andretti's car had broken down, he had won the Austrian and Japanese Grand Prix and had finished strongly in many

At the 1979 IROC race at Riverside, California, Andretti battles with Emerson Fittipaldi.

other races. Now, with only four races left in the season, the number two driver on the Lotus team had 45 points and was in a position to win the season championship himself.

At the Holland Grand Prix, Andretti finally found himself behind the wheel of the Lotus 79. He had no choice because he had crashed the older Lotus two weeks earlier at the Austrian Grand Prix. The Lotus 79 was a gem, and Mario captured the pole position. On race day, Mario zoomed off and built up a comfortable lead. Peterson, running in second place, continued to be the consummate team player. Although he had several opportunities to challenge Andretti for the lead, he concentrated on keeping Reutemann and Lauda off Andretti's tail. Mario charged to the finish line, capturing the checkered flag and nine more precious Grand Prix points. He also took one giant step toward becoming the first American to win the Grand Prix points championship since Phil Hill had won it in 1961.

Andretti could capture the championship at the September 10th race in Monza, Italy. Mario won the pole position, and when the green flag fell, he pushed the Lotus 79 into the lead. Behind him, however, disaster had struck. Seconds into the race, a fiery 10-car pile-up had erupted. Ronnie Peterson, starting in the fifth slot, was among the drivers involved. The race was stopped while all of the twisted wreckage was removed from the course. An ambulance rushed Peterson to the hospital. Preliminary reports indicated that he had suffered multiple leg injuries, from which the doctors felt certain that he would recover. The race was restarted after a three-hour delay, and Andretti cruised around the course and sped across the finish line in first place.

When Andretti walked to the judge's stand to claim the Monza Cup, he learned that he and the second-place finisher, Gilles Villeneuve of Canada, were being penalized one minute for starting too early at the restart of the race. The judges gave third-place finisher Lauda the winner's trophy. Mario soon learned that even though he did not win the race, he had clinched the season title. Because of his injuries, Peterson would miss the final two races of the season.

Andretti's mixed emotions—being stripped of the victory in Italy's most important race but capturing the season championship anyway—were throw into absolute chaos the next morning. Despite the early optimistic prognosis, Peterson slipped into a coma and died of kidney failure as a result of the crash. Mario was devastated. He and Peterson had been good friends and model teammates. When asked about winning the Grand Prix championship the following day, Andretti responded, "This is no time to think about celebrating. I just can't begin to talk about the championship at this stage. We worked so hard, so close together this year, to make it all happen, and now it seems a kind of hollow victory."

People in the racing world tried to comfort Andretti. Veteran driver and car owner Dan Gurney wrote, "Well done, Champ. If any Formula 1 Grand Prix Driver deserves the title World Champion, you get my vote and congratulations." Phil Hill, the American driver who had won the Grand Prix championship in 1961, sent a telegram that read, "Sincere congratulations on attaining your dream of world champion after a hard-fought and honorable climb to the title."

After winning the Formula 1 championship, Andretti kept doing what he did best—racing.

The victories, however, began to occur with less frequency. Mario continued to drive on the Formula 1 circuit, winning the Meadowlands Grand Prix in 1984 and the Long Beach Grand Prix in 1985.

But at the same time, his bad luck at Indy continued. In 1981, track officials awarded him the victory when first-place finisher Bobby Unser was penalized for passing cars under a yellow flag. Unser appealed the ruling, which was eventually reversed, and Andretti's victory was taken away. The following year, Mario found himself in the cockpit of a hot car, but a crash at the start of the race knocked him out of the race. His teammate, Gordon Johncock, captured the checkered flag—in an identical car.

In 1985, Andretti avoided the spinning car of the leader, Danny Sullivan, and led Indy for 102 laps. Sullivan managed not to hit anything in his spin, and he came back to take the lead from Mario and win the race. Andretti finished in second place again—so close to his second Indy win, yet so far away. In 1987, Andretti had led the race for 170 laps when his engine failed. In 1993, Mario was in the hunt for the victory once again. He led for 72 laps, but a bad tire dropped him to a fifth-place finish.

Before the 1994 season, Mario Andretti announced that it would be his last as a race car driver. At about the same time, *Car and Driver* magazine named him as one of the top 10 American drivers of all time. As the 54-year-old veteran took his final spins around the racetracks of the world, fans got their last glimpses at the racing legend. The winner of three USAC national championships and a Formula 1 world championship, Andretti had scored victories on a wide array of tracks in a wide variety of cars. He won sprint car and midget races on dirt tracks, stock car races on paved ovals, championship and road races in Indy cars, endurance races in sports cars, and Grand Prix races in Formula 1 cars.

As he prepared for retirement, Andretti also readied himself to pass along a rich tradition to a younger generation of racing Andrettis. His sons, Michael and Jeff, have followed in their father's footsteps, becoming world-class drivers in their own rights. Mario's nephew, John, has also become a respected driver. The racing world has long been dominated by such family dynasties as the Unsers, Foyts, Pettys, Allisons, Vukoviches, and Bettenhausens. Of all these families, the Andrettis have been the most successful.

Although Mario's accomplishments would satisfy many racing families, the young Andrettis want to keep the Andretti name in Victory Lane. Michael claimed his first USAC national championship in 1991 at age 28 but was not satisfied with that feat. Having watched his father compete on the exciting Formula 1 circuit, Michael is now striving to become the first son of a Formula 1 champion to win that title also. Jeff Andretti, who is one year younger than Michael, was the 1991 Rookie of the Year at Indy. Although not as successful as Michael so far, Jeff hopes to make a name for himself. Aldo's son, John, is also carrying on the Andretti tradition. He won the first Indy Car race of the 1991 season at Surfer's Paradise, Australia.

The 1992 USAC season proved to be an exceptional showcase for the Andrettis. At every Indy car race that year, four Andrettis were in the field.

All four qualified for the Indy 500—an incredible feat because only 33 drivers can qualify for the race. Two years later, Mario and Michael Andretti shared a special moment. At the 1994 Australian Indy Car Grand Prix, the Andrettis finished first and third. Michael won the race, but his proud father showed everyone that the old man still had something left in his tank.

In a 1978 interview, Mario perhaps best summed up what drove him to race: "My goal

Michael Andretti (left) manages a smile after Dad beat him in the Portland (Oregon) Rose Festival Cart 200 on Father's Day, 1986. Michael ran out of gas on the backstretch of the last lap, allowing Mario to win by the minuscule margin of seven-hundreths of a second.

has been to win in every category of racing. To smoke them all where they least expect me to. I have won on 127 different kinds of tracks, clockwise and counterclockwise. I have experienced the passing of the engine from the front to the back. I have raced with the greats who have since retired, and in places that are now parking lots. So I'm an old fogy, but how many guys have done all that?"

As older drivers pass the torch to a new generation of drivers, some racing fans doubt that the younger stars will ever attain the legendary status of Mario Andretti, A. J. Foyt, Al and Bobby Unser, Richard Petty, and the other great names in racing. In an era of large financial payoffs for winning races, camaraderie and trust among drivers have diminished. Auto racing seems to boast fewer original personalities, and much of the romance of the sport seems to have faded. But what will never fade are the accomplishments of the man who could win any kind of race, Mario Andretti.

STATISTICS

Highlights of Mario Andretti's championship seasons:

1965 USAC CHAMPIONSHIP

Date	Track	Distance	Finish
April 25	Trenton	100	2
May 31	Indianapolis	500	3
June 20	Langhorne	100	2
July 25	Indianapolis Raceway Park	150	1
August 1	Atlanta	300	2
August 14	Milwaukee	150	2
August 21	Springfield	100	3
September 18	Indianapolis Fairgrounds	100	2
October 24	Sacramento	100	3
November 11	Phoenix	200	2

1966 USAC CHAMPIONSHIP

Date	Track	Distance	Finish
June 5	Milwaukee	100	1
June 12	Langhorne	100	1
June 26	Atlanta	300	1
July 24	Indianapolis Raceway Park	150	1
August 20	Springfield	100	2
August 27	Milwaukee	200	1
September 10	Indianapolis Fairgrounds	100	1
September 25	Trenton	200	1
November 20	Phoenix	200	1

1969 USAC CHAMPIONSHIP

Date	Track	Distance	Finish
April 13	Hanford	200	1
May 30	Indianapolis	500	1
June 29	Pike's Peak	12.5	1
July 19	Trenton	200	1
July 27	Indianapolis Raceway Park	100	2
August 18	Springfield	100	1
September 1	DuQuoin	100	2
September 21	Trenton	300	1
December 7	Riverside	300	1

1978 FORMULA 1 CHAMPIONSHIP

Date	Event, Site	Finish
January	Argentina Grand Prix, Buenos Aires	1
April	Spanish G.P., Jarama	1
May	Belgium G.P., Spa-Fransorchamps	1
July	French G.P., LeMans	1
August	Holland G.P., Zandvoort	1
September	Italian G.P., Monza	3

MARIO ANDRETTI
A CHRONOLOGY

1940   Mario and brother Aldo born on February 28 in Montona, Italy

1948   The Andrettis leave Montona (Motovun, Yugoslavia); repatriate to Italy; settle in refugee camp

1955   The Andrettis arrive in the United States on June 16

1959   Mario and Aldo begin racing at Nazareth Speedway

1961   Mario marries Dee Ann Hoch on November 25

1964   Wins first USAC race, a 100-mile sprint race at Salem, IN; becomes U.S. citizen on April 15

1965   Wins USAC national points championship; named "Rookie of the Year" at Indianapolis 500

1966   Wins second USAC national championship

1967   Finishes second in USAC national championship; wins Daytona 500 and 12 Hours at Sebring endurance race

1968   Finishes second in USAC national championship; drives in first Formula 1 race

1969   Wins third USAC national championship; wins Indy 500

1970   Wins second 12 Hours at Sebring

1971   Wins two Formula 1 races

1976   Wins Japanese Grand Prix

1977   Wins four Formula 1 races

1978   Wins six Formula 1 races and the Grand Prix points championship

1981   Awarded Indy 500 victory when judges strip Bobby Unser of title; awarded second after Unser's successful appeal

1984   Wins Meadowlands Grand Prix

1985   Finishes second at Indy 500; wins Long Beach Grand Prix

1992   Four Andrettis—Mario, Michael, Jeff, and John—qualify for Indy 500

1994   Mario Andretti retires from racing

SUGGESTIONS FOR FURTHER READING

Andretti, Mario. *What's It Like Out There?* Chicago: Henry Regnery Co., 1970.

Andretti, Michael. *Michael Andretti at Indianapolis.* New York: Simon & Schuster, 1993.

Associated Press Sports Staff. *A Century of Champions.* New York: Macmillan, 1976.

Engel, Lyle Kenyon. *Mario Andretti.* New York: Arco, 1979.

———. *Road Racing in America.* New York: Dodd, Mead, 1971.

Hinton, Ed. "Inherit the Wind." *Sports Illustrated*, May 11, 1992.

Jezierski, Chet. *Speed: Indy Car Racing.* New York: Abrams, 1992.

Leifer, Neil. *Neil Leifer's Sports Stars.* Garden City, N.Y.: Dolphin Books, 1985.

Libby, Bill. *Andretti: The Story of Auto-Racing's Toughest, Most Versatile and Courageous Driver.* New York: Grosset & Dunlap, 1970.

Roebuck, Nigel. *Grand Prix Greats.* Wellingborough, U.K.: Patrick Stevens, 1986.

Sutton, Stan. "Destiny's Darling Andretti Ain't." *The Sporting News*, June 1, 1987.

ABOUT THE AUTHOR

G. S. Prentzas is an editor and writer who lives in New York City. He has written eight books for young readers, including a guide to the 1994 Winter Olympics and a biography of football legend Jim Brown.

INDEX

PICTURE CREDITS
Courtesy Indy Car: 2; UPI/Bettmann: 8, 24, 43, 50, 52, 59; Bob Tronolone, Burbank, CA: 11, 36,
44, 54; Bruce Craig Photos, Phillipsburg, NJ: 14, 20, 28, 33, 35, 40, 47.

9|05   2   5|01

8|12   2   —

8|17   3   3|17

12|19   4   2|19

4|21   4   2|19

1|23   4   2|19

DEMCO